EMMANUEL JOSEPH

Champions of Code, How AI and Mythology Inspire the Evolution of Sports

Copyright © 2025 by Emmanuel Joseph

All rights reserved. No part of this publication may be reproduced, stored or transmitted in any form or by any means, electronic, mechanical, photocopying, recording, scanning, or otherwise without written permission from the publisher. It is illegal to copy this book, post it to a website, or distribute it by any other means without permission.

First edition

This book was professionally typeset on Reedsy.
Find out more at reedsy.com

Contents

1

Chapter 1: The Dawn of AI in Sports

Artificial Intelligence (AI) has transformed sports in unimaginable ways. Historically, sports have always been about physical prowess and human skill. However, the integration of AI has introduced a new era where data-driven decisions enhance performance, strategy, and even fan engagement. From wearable technology to advanced analytics, AI is revolutionizing how athletes train and how teams compete. AI's predictive algorithms can analyze an athlete's performance, highlight areas for improvement, and suggest optimal training regimens. This fusion of technology and sports is pushing the boundaries of human capabilities.

In addition to performance enhancement, AI is also making significant strides in injury prevention and recovery. Through the analysis of biomechanical data, AI systems can identify potential injury risks before they occur. For instance, motion capture technology combined with AI algorithms can detect subtle changes in an athlete's movements, flagging potential issues that might lead to injuries. This proactive approach not only helps athletes stay in peak condition but also extends their careers. The integration of AI in sports medicine is proving to be a game-changer.

Moreover, AI is transforming the fan experience. With the advent of virtual and augmented reality, fans can now immerse themselves in the game like never before. AI-driven platforms provide real-time statistics, player profiles, and even predict game outcomes, enhancing the overall viewing experience.

The use of AI in sports broadcasting is revolutionizing how fans consume sports, making it more interactive and engaging. As AI continues to evolve, its impact on the sports industry will only grow, ushering in a new era of innovation.

Lastly, the ethical implications of AI in sports cannot be overlooked. As AI systems become more integrated into sports, questions about data privacy, fairness, and the potential for misuse arise. It is crucial to establish ethical guidelines to ensure that AI is used responsibly and transparently. The collaboration between technologists, athletes, and regulatory bodies will be essential in navigating these challenges. The dawn of AI in sports marks a significant milestone, but it is only the beginning of a transformative journey.

2

Chapter 2: The Mythological Connection

Throughout history, mythology has played a significant role in shaping human culture and beliefs. Stories of gods and heroes have inspired generations, offering lessons in courage, perseverance, and the quest for greatness. In many ways, the narratives of mythology mirror the journey of athletes in the world of sports. The challenges, triumphs, and sacrifices faced by mythological figures resonate with the experiences of modern-day sports champions. By exploring the connections between mythology and sports, we gain a deeper understanding of the human spirit and the pursuit of excellence.

One of the most iconic mythological figures that resonate with the world of sports is Hercules. Known for his incredible strength and heroic deeds, Hercules' twelve labors symbolize the relentless pursuit of greatness. Just as Hercules faced seemingly insurmountable challenges, athletes push their limits to achieve their goals. The story of Hercules serves as a powerful metaphor for the dedication, resilience, and determination required to succeed in sports. It reminds us that the path to greatness is often fraught with obstacles, but with unwavering resolve, anything is possible.

Another compelling connection between mythology and sports can be found in the story of Athena, the goddess of wisdom and strategy. Athena's strategic brilliance and tactical acumen mirror the importance of strategy and planning in sports. Whether it's a coach devising game plans or an athlete making split-second decisions, the principles of strategy and intelligence are paramount. The mythological figure of Athena serves as a reminder that success in sports is not solely dependent on physical prowess but also on mental agility and strategic thinking.

The influence of mythology on sports extends beyond individual figures to entire cultures. For instance, the ancient Olympic Games were deeply rooted in Greek mythology, dedicated to the gods and held in honor of Zeus. The spirit of the Olympic Games embodies the values of unity, competition, and the pursuit of excellence. The mythological origins of the Olympics highlight the timeless connection between sports and the celebration of human potential. By drawing inspiration from these ancient stories, modern athletes and sports enthusiasts can find a sense of purpose and motivation.

3

Chapter 3: The Evolution of Training Techniques

The evolution of training techniques in sports is a testament to the continuous quest for improvement and excellence. Over the years, training methods have undergone significant transformations, influenced by advancements in technology, scientific research, and innovative approaches. From traditional practices rooted in discipline and repetition to cutting-edge techniques that leverage AI and data analytics, the journey of training evolution is a fascinating one. This chapter explores the key milestones and innovations that have shaped the way athletes train and prepare for competition.

In the early days of sports, training methods were primarily based on intuition and experience. Coaches relied on their knowledge and observations to design training programs. While this approach produced remarkable athletes, it lacked the precision and scientific rigor that modern training techniques offer. The advent of sports science marked a turning point, introducing a systematic and evidence-based approach to training. Concepts such as periodization, biomechanics, and sports nutrition revolutionized how athletes prepared for competition, optimizing performance and reducing the risk of injuries.

The integration of AI in training techniques has taken the quest for excellence to new heights. AI-driven platforms analyze vast amounts of data, providing insights into an athlete's performance, strengths, and weaknesses. This data-driven approach allows for personalized training programs tailored to individual needs. Wearable devices equipped with sensors track metrics such as heart rate, movement patterns, and muscle activity in real-time. AI algorithms process this data to offer actionable feedback, enabling athletes to make informed decisions and continuously improve their performance.

One of the most notable advancements in training techniques is the use of virtual reality (VR) and augmented reality (AR). These immersive technologies provide athletes with realistic simulations, allowing them to practice and refine their skills in a controlled environment. For example, VR can recreate game scenarios, helping athletes develop situational awareness and decision-making abilities. AR, on the other hand, overlays digital information onto the physical world, offering real-time guidance and corrections. The combination of VR and AR with AI opens up new possibilities for training, making it more engaging and effective.

As training techniques continue to evolve, the importance of mental preparation and psychological resilience is increasingly recognized. Sports psychology plays a crucial role in helping athletes develop mental toughness, focus, and confidence. Techniques such as visualization, mindfulness, and cognitive-behavioral strategies are integrated into training programs to enhance mental performance. The holistic approach to training, which encompasses physical, technical, and psychological aspects, ensures that athletes are well-prepared to face the challenges of competition. The evolution of training techniques is a testament to the relentless pursuit of excellence in sports.

4

Chapter 4: The Role of Data Analytics

Data analytics has become an integral part of the sports industry, revolutionizing how teams strategize, coaches make decisions, and athletes optimize their performance. The ability to collect, process, and analyze vast amounts of data provides valuable insights that were previously unimaginable. From tracking player movements to analyzing game statistics, data analytics offers a competitive edge in the world of sports. This chapter explores the various applications of data analytics in sports and how it is transforming the industry.

One of the most significant contributions of data analytics is in player performance analysis. By capturing detailed data on an athlete's movements, actions, and biometrics, coaches and analysts can gain a comprehensive understanding of their performance. Metrics such as speed, agility, and endurance are quantified and visualized, allowing for precise evaluation and improvement. Data analytics also enables the identification of patterns and trends, helping athletes and coaches make informed decisions to enhance performance and reduce the risk of injuries.

In addition to individual performance analysis, data analytics plays a crucial role in team strategy and game planning. By analyzing historical game data, teams can identify strengths, weaknesses, and tendencies of both their own players and their opponents. This information is used to devise game plans, optimize lineups, and develop tactics that maximize the chances of success.

For example, in basketball, data analytics can determine the most effective shot locations and defensive strategies, leading to more efficient play and better results.

The use of data analytics extends beyond performance and strategy to fan engagement and experience. Sports organizations leverage data to understand fan behavior, preferences, and engagement patterns. This information is used to tailor marketing efforts, enhance fan experiences, and increase revenue. For instance, data analytics can identify the most popular merchandise items, the best times to send promotional offers, and the most engaging content for social media. By leveraging data, sports organizations can create personalized and immersive experiences that keep fans connected and invested in the game.

Moreover, data analytics is driving innovation in sports technology and equipment. Wearable devices, smart clothing, and IoT sensors are designed to collect and transmit data in real-time. This data is analyzed to provide insights into performance, recovery, and overall health. Advanced algorithms and machine learning models continuously improve the accuracy and reliability of these devices. The integration of data analytics with sports technology is pushing the boundaries of what is possible, enabling athletes to achieve new levels of performance and excellence.

5

Chapter 5: AI Coaches and Virtual Assistants

The concept of AI coaches and virtual assistants is no longer a futuristic dream but a reality transforming the landscape of sports. AI-powered coaches provide personalized training, feedback, and support, helping athletes optimize their performance and achieve their goals. These virtual assistants are equipped with advanced algorithms that analyze data, identify areas for improvement, and offer actionable recommendations. This chapter delves into the rise of AI coaches and virtual assistants and their impact on the sports industry.

AI coaches utilize data from various sources, including wearable devices, video footage, and biometric sensors, to create detailed profiles of athletes. By analyzing this data, AI coaches can identify strengths, weaknesses, and patterns in an athlete's performance. They provide real-time feedback and suggestions, enabling athletes to make adjustments and improvements during training sessions. The personalized nature of AI coaching ensures that athletes receive targeted and effective guidance, tailored to their unique needs and goals.

Virtual assistants, on the other hand, offer a range of support services that extend beyond training. These AI-powered companions can assist athletes with scheduling, nutrition planning, mental health support, and more. By integrating data from various aspects of an athlete's life, virtual assistants provide a holistic approach to performance optimization. They can remind athletes of important appointments, suggest meal plans based on dietary needs, and even offer motivational messages to boost morale. The convenience and comprehensive support provided by virtual assistants make them invaluable tools in an athlete's journey.

The benefits of AI coaches and virtual assistants are not limited to professional athletes. Amateur and recreational athletes can also take advantage of these technologies to enhance their training and overall experience. AI-powered fitness apps, for example, offer personalized workout plans, track progress, and provide feedback, making fitness more accessible and enjoyable for everyone. The democratization of AI in sports ensures that athletes of all levels can benefit from the same advanced tools and insights.

As AI coaches and virtual assistants become more sophisticated, the collaboration between human coaches and AI systems is becoming increasingly seamless. Human coaches can leverage AI-generated insights to fine-tune their training programs and make more informed decisions. The combination of human intuition and AI precision creates a powerful synergy that maximizes the potential of athletes. This collaborative approach ensures that the human touch remains an essential component of coaching, while AI enhances and augments the process.

However, the rise of AI coaches and virtual assistants also raises important ethical and practical considerations. Issues such as data privacy, the potential for over-reliance on technology, and the need for transparency in AI decision-making processes must be addressed. It is crucial to strike a balance between leveraging AI's capabilities and preserving the human elements of coaching and support. By navigating these challenges thoughtfully, the sports industry can harness the full potential of AI while ensuring that athletes' best interests are always at the forefront.

6

Chapter 6: Mythological Figures as Role Models

Mythological figures have long been celebrated as symbols of strength, wisdom, and virtue. Their stories continue to inspire and resonate with people across generations. In the realm of sports, these figures serve as powerful role models, embodying qualities that athletes strive to emulate. This chapter explores the impact of mythological figures as role models and how their timeless stories influence the values and aspirations of modern athletes.

One of the most iconic mythological figures that athletes look up to is Achilles, the legendary Greek hero known for his unparalleled strength and bravery. Achilles' unwavering determination and resilience in the face of adversity resonate with athletes who are constantly pushing their limits. His story reminds athletes that true greatness requires not only physical prowess but also mental fortitude and an indomitable spirit. The legacy of Achilles serves as a source of motivation and inspiration for athletes seeking to achieve their own heroic feats.

Another influential mythological figure is Artemis, the Greek goddess of the hunt and wilderness. Artemis embodies qualities such as independence, focus, and mastery of her craft. Her connection to nature and her unwavering commitment to her goals inspire athletes to stay disciplined and dedicated to their training. The story of Artemis highlights the importance of balance and harmony with the natural world, encouraging athletes to find their own equilibrium and maintain a holistic approach to their pursuits.

The influence of mythological figures extends beyond individual attributes to encompass broader cultural values. For example, the ancient Norse gods, with their tales of valor, honor, and camaraderie, resonate deeply with team sports. The camaraderie and unity displayed by figures such as Thor and Odin mirror the dynamics of a successful sports team. These mythological narratives emphasize the significance of teamwork, loyalty, and collective effort in achieving greatness. Athletes draw inspiration from these stories, fostering a sense of camaraderie and shared purpose within their teams.

Mythological figures also offer valuable lessons in humility and the acceptance of one's limitations. The story of Icarus, who flew too close to the sun with his wax wings and fell to his demise, serves as a cautionary tale against hubris and overconfidence. Athletes are reminded that while ambition and determination are essential, it is equally important to recognize one's limitations and approach challenges with humility. The myth of Icarus encourages athletes to strive for greatness while remaining grounded and aware of their own vulnerabilities.

7

Chapter 7: The Future of AI in Sports

The future of AI in sports holds immense potential for innovation and transformation. As technology continues to advance, the integration of AI will further revolutionize the way athletes train, compete, and engage with fans. This chapter explores the exciting possibilities that lie ahead and the emerging trends that are set to shape the future of AI in the sports industry.

One of the most promising areas of development is the use of AI in predictive analytics. AI algorithms can analyze vast amounts of historical data to identify patterns and trends, enabling more accurate predictions of game outcomes and player performance. This capability has significant implications for sports betting, fantasy sports, and strategic decision-making by coaches and teams. The ability to anticipate and adapt to future scenarios will give teams a competitive edge and enhance the overall strategy and planning process.

AI is also expected to play a crucial role in the development of smart sports equipment and facilities. Innovations such as AI-powered stadiums with advanced sensors and automation systems will enhance the fan experience and optimize operational efficiency. Smart equipment, including AI-integrated wearables and training devices, will provide real-time feedback and insights, helping athletes fine-tune their performance. The fusion of AI with sports infrastructure and equipment will create a more immersive, efficient, and data-driven environment.

Another exciting frontier for AI in sports is the exploration of virtual and augmented reality. These immersive technologies, combined with AI, will offer new ways for athletes to train and for fans to experience sports. Virtual reality simulations can recreate realistic game scenarios, allowing athletes to practice and improve their skills in a controlled environment. Augmented reality can enhance live sports broadcasts by overlaying real-time data and interactive content, creating a more engaging and informative viewing experience. The convergence of AI, VR, and AR will redefine the boundaries of sports training and entertainment.

As AI continues to evolve, ethical considerations will remain a key focus. Ensuring data privacy, fairness, and transparency in AI decision-making processes will be essential to maintaining trust and integrity in the sports industry. Collaboration between technologists, athletes, regulatory bodies, and stakeholders will be crucial in establishing guidelines and standards for the responsible use of AI. By addressing these challenges proactively, the sports industry can harness the full potential of AI while safeguarding the interests and well-being of all stakeholders.

8

Chapter 8: The Cultural Impact of Sports and Mythology

Sports and mythology have long been intertwined, shaping cultures and societies throughout history. The narratives of mythological figures and the achievements of sports champions resonate deeply with people, transcending geographical and cultural boundaries. This chapter explores the cultural impact of sports and mythology, highlighting how these powerful influences continue to inspire and unite communities around the world.

In many cultures, sports serve as a unifying force, bringing people together in celebration of human potential and achievement. The spirit of competition and the pursuit of excellence are values that resonate universally. Sports events, such as the Olympic Games and the FIFA World Cup, capture the imagination of millions, fostering a sense of global community and shared experience. The stories of athletes who overcome challenges and achieve greatness become cultural touchstones, inspiring future generations to dream big and strive for excellence.

Mythology, too, has a profound impact on cultural identity and values. The tales of gods, heroes, and mythical creatures reflect the beliefs, aspirations, and moral codes of societies. These stories offer timeless lessons in courage, wisdom, and resilience, shaping the character and values of individuals and communities. The mythological narratives that have endured through the ages continue to inspire contemporary culture, influencing literature, art, and even sports.

The intersection of sports and mythology can be seen in the rituals and traditions associated with athletic events. Many sports ceremonies and practices draw inspiration from mythological themes, paying homage to the gods and heroes of the past. For example, the lighting of the Olympic torch is a symbolic act that traces its origins to ancient Greece, honoring the mythological significance of fire as a source of life and inspiration. These rituals connect the present with the past, creating a sense of continuity and reverence for tradition.

The cultural impact of sports and mythology extends to the realm of education and personal development. The stories of mythological figures and sports champions serve as powerful educational tools, teaching important life lessons and values. Schools and educational programs often incorporate these narratives into their curricula, using them to inspire and motivate students. The themes of perseverance, teamwork, and integrity that are central to both sports and mythology resonate deeply with young minds, shaping their character and guiding their actions.

9

Chapter 9: The Intersection of Technology and Tradition

The intersection of technology and tradition in sports and mythology is a fascinating and dynamic space. As AI and other advanced technologies continue to evolve, they are reshaping traditional practices and narratives in both fields. This chapter explores how technology is transforming the way we engage with sports and mythology while preserving the essence and values that define them.

In the world of sports, technology has revolutionized training, performance analysis, and fan engagement. However, it is essential to strike a balance between embracing innovation and preserving the traditions that make sports meaningful. For example, while AI-powered analytics provide valuable insights, the human element of coaching and mentorship remains irreplaceable. The wisdom, experience, and emotional support that human coaches offer are integral to an athlete's development. The challenge lies in integrating technology in a way that enhances rather than replaces these traditional aspects.

Similarly, the integration of technology into the realm of mythology offers new ways to experience and interpret ancient stories. Virtual reality and augmented reality can bring mythological narratives to life, allowing people to immerse themselves in the worlds of gods and heroes. Digital platforms provide access to a wealth of mythological content, making it more accessible to a global audience. However, it is important to ensure that these technological innovations respect and preserve the cultural and historical significance of mythological traditions.

In preserving the cultural and historical significance of mythological traditions, it is crucial to maintain the authenticity and integrity of these ancient stories. Technology can serve as a bridge between the past and the present, making mythological narratives more accessible while respecting their original context. Digital archives and online platforms allow people to explore and learn about mythology from different cultures, fostering a greater appreciation and understanding of these timeless stories. By leveraging technology responsibly, we can ensure that the essence of mythology is preserved for future generations.

In the world of sports, the integration of technology must also be balanced with the preservation of tradition. The rituals, ceremonies, and cultural practices associated with sports events are integral to their significance. For instance, the pre-match haka performed by New Zealand's rugby team is a powerful cultural tradition that embodies the spirit and identity of the team. While technology can enhance the performance and experience of sports, it is essential to honor and respect these traditions. By finding a harmonious balance between innovation and tradition, we can create a richer and more meaningful sports experience.

The intersection of technology and tradition also offers opportunities for cultural exchange and collaboration. Global sports events bring together athletes and fans from diverse backgrounds, fostering a sense of unity and mutual respect. Technology can facilitate this exchange by providing platforms for cross-cultural dialogue and interaction. For example, virtual reality experiences can transport fans to different parts of the world, allowing them to experience the cultural nuances of sports events in other countries. This cultural exchange enriches our understanding and appreciation of the diverse traditions that shape the world of sports.

In conclusion, the intersection of technology and tradition in sports and mythology is a dynamic and evolving space. By embracing innovation while preserving the essence of these fields, we can create a more enriched and meaningful experience. The responsible integration of technology ensures that the values, stories, and traditions that define sports and mythology are respected and cherished. As we navigate this intersection, we have the opportunity to celebrate the best of both worlds and inspire future generations to explore the possibilities that lie ahead.

10

Chapter 10: The Power of Storytelling

Storytelling is a fundamental human activity that has the power to inspire, educate, and connect people. In the realms of sports and mythology, storytelling plays a pivotal role in shaping narratives, values, and identities. This chapter explores the significance of storytelling in sports and mythology, highlighting how these narratives continue to impact and influence individuals and communities.

In sports, storytelling is often centered around the journeys of athletes, teams, and memorable moments. The stories of triumphs, defeats, comebacks, and records create a rich tapestry that captivates fans and transcends the boundaries of the game. These narratives celebrate the dedication, resilience, and passion of athletes, turning them into heroes and role models. The power of storytelling in sports lies in its ability to evoke emotions, build connections, and inspire people to strive for greatness.

Mythology, on the other hand, is a repository of ancient stories that convey cultural values, beliefs, and wisdom. The mythological narratives of gods, heroes, and mythical creatures offer timeless lessons in courage, morality, and the human condition. These stories have been passed down through generations, preserving the cultural heritage and identity of societies. The power of mythological storytelling lies in its universality and ability to resonate with people across different cultures and time periods.

The convergence of sports and mythology in storytelling creates a unique and compelling narrative landscape. The values and themes that emerge from mythological stories often find parallels in the world of sports. The quest for glory, the struggle against adversity, and the celebration of human potential are common threads that weave together these narratives. By drawing inspiration from both sports and mythology, storytellers can create powerful and impactful narratives that inspire and motivate.

The advent of digital media and technology has expanded the reach and impact of storytelling in sports and mythology. Social media platforms, streaming services, and digital content have made it easier to share and access stories from around the world. This democratization of storytelling allows for a diverse range of voices and perspectives to be heard. Fans can connect with athletes, share their own stories, and engage in conversations that transcend geographical boundaries. The digital age has given rise to a new era of storytelling, where the narratives of sports and mythology can reach and inspire a global audience.

11

Chapter 11: The Role of Innovation in Sports

Innovation is the driving force behind the continuous evolution and advancement of sports. From the development of new training techniques to the introduction of cutting-edge technologies, innovation shapes the way athletes compete, train, and engage with fans. This chapter explores the role of innovation in sports, highlighting key advancements and their impact on the industry.

One of the most significant innovations in sports is the use of advanced analytics and data science. The ability to collect and analyze vast amounts of data has revolutionized how teams strategize, coaches make decisions, and athletes optimize their performance. Metrics such as player movements, shot accuracy, and physiological data provide valuable insights that inform training and game planning. The use of data analytics has become an essential tool for gaining a competitive edge and enhancing overall performance.

In addition to analytics, wearable technology has become a game-changer in sports innovation. Devices such as fitness trackers, smartwatches, and biometric sensors provide real-time data on an athlete's performance and health. These wearables track metrics such as heart rate, sleep patterns, and movement, allowing athletes to monitor their progress and make informed decisions. The integration of AI with wearable technology enhances the accuracy and reliability of these devices, providing personalized feedback and recommendations.

Virtual and augmented reality are also playing a significant role in sports innovation. These immersive technologies offer new ways for athletes to train and for fans to experience sports. Virtual reality simulations provide realistic game scenarios, helping athletes develop situational awareness and decision-making skills. Augmented reality enhances live sports broadcasts by overlaying real-time data and interactive content, creating a more engaging and informative viewing experience. The combination of VR, AR, and AI is transforming the way athletes train and fans consume sports.

Innovation in sports is not limited to technology but also encompasses advancements in sports medicine and recovery. Techniques such as cryotherapy, regenerative medicine, and biomechanical analysis are revolutionizing how athletes recover from injuries and optimize their performance. AI-powered systems analyze biomechanical data to identify potential injury risks and provide targeted interventions. The integration of technology with sports medicine ensures that athletes can maintain peak performance and extend their careers.

12

Chapter 12: The Legacy of AI and Mythology in Sports

As we look to the future, the legacy of AI and mythology in sports will continue to shape the industry in profound ways. The integration of AI has already revolutionized training, performance analysis, and fan engagement, pushing the boundaries of what is possible. Meanwhile, the timeless stories of mythology continue to inspire and motivate athletes, offering valuable lessons in resilience, courage, and the pursuit of excellence.

The legacy of AI in sports is characterized by its ability to enhance and optimize every aspect of the athletic experience. From personalized training programs to advanced analytics, AI provides tools that empower athletes to reach their full potential. The impact of AI extends beyond individual athletes to entire teams and organizations, transforming how sports are played, managed, and enjoyed. As AI technology continues to evolve, its legacy will be defined by its contribution to the continuous improvement and innovation of the sports industry.

The influence of mythology in sports is equally enduring. The stories of gods, heroes, and mythical creatures offer timeless lessons that resonate with athletes and fans alike. These narratives provide a sense of purpose and inspiration, reminding us of the values and virtues that define human excellence. The legacy of mythology in sports is reflected in the enduring spirit of competition, the pursuit of greatness, and the celebration of human potential. As we move forward, the stories of mythology will continue to guide and inspire the next generation of athletes.

The convergence of AI and mythology in sports creates a unique and powerful synergy. AI provides the tools and technologies that enhance performance and innovation, while mythology offers the narratives and values that inspire and motivate. Together, they shape the future of sports, creating a rich and dynamic landscape that celebrates both human potential and technological advancement. The legacy of AI and mythology in sports is a testament to the enduring power of innovation and storytelling.

In conclusion, "Champions of Code: How AI and Mythology Inspire the Evolution of Sports" explores the transformative impact of AI and mythology on the world of sports. From the dawn of AI integration to the timeless influence of mythological narratives, this book highlights the ways in which these powerful forces shape the journey of athletes and the sports industry as a whole. As we look to the future, the legacy of AI and mythology will continue to inspire, innovate, and elevate the world of sports, celebrating the best of human potential and technological advancement.

The book description

In "Champions of Code: How AI and Mythology Inspire the Evolution of Sports," we embark on an exploration of how artificial intelligence and ancient mythological stories intersect to shape the future of sports. This book delves into the transformative impact of AI, from revolutionizing training techniques and performance analytics to enhancing fan experiences with immersive technologies. It also examines the timeless influence of mythology, drawing parallels between the heroic journeys of mythological figures and the challenges faced by modern athletes.

Through twelve engaging chapters, readers will discover how AI coaches provide personalized training, how data analytics drives strategic decisions, and how virtual reality brings game scenarios to life. The book also highlights the cultural significance of mythology in sports, offering valuable lessons in resilience, strategy, and the pursuit of excellence. As AI and mythology converge, they create a powerful synergy that inspires and elevates the world of sports, celebrating both human potential and technological advancement.

"Champions of Code" is a compelling narrative that celebrates the legacy of AI and mythology in sports, offering insights into the future of athletic innovation and the enduring power of storytelling. This book is a must-read for anyone fascinated by the intersection of technology, culture, and the human spirit in the realm of sports.

www.ingramcontent.com/pod-product-compliance
Lightning Source LLC
Chambersburg PA
CBHW051014050726
47592CB00007B/2844